Reading

BOROUGH COUNCIL

Reading Borough Libraries

Email: info@readinglibraries.org.uk
Website: www.readinglibraries.org.uk

Reading 0118 9015950
Battle 0118 9015100
Caversham 0118 9015103
Palmer Park 0118 9015106
Southcote 0118 9015109
Tilehurst 0118 9015112
Whitley 0118 9015115

JOHNSON, Jinny   PET
Sea Lion
CH599.7975

CHILDREN'S LIBRARY

To avoid overdue charges please return this book to a
Reading library on or before the last date stamped above.
If not required by another reader, it may be renewed by
personal visit, telephone, post, email, or via our website.

ZOO ANIMALS
IN THE WILD

SEA LION

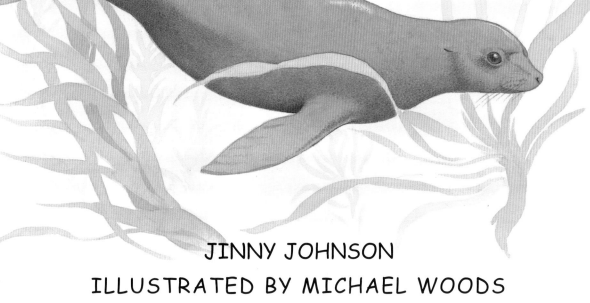

JINNY JOHNSON
ILLUSTRATED BY MICHAEL WOODS

W
FRANKLIN WATTS
LONDON•SYDNEY

 An Appleseed Editions book

First published in 2006 by Franklin Watts
338 Euston Road, London NW1 3BH

Franklin Watts Australia, Hachette Children's Books
Level 17/207 Kent Street, Sydney, NSW 2000

© 2006 Appleseed Editions

Created by Appleseed Editions Ltd, Well House,
Friars Hill, Guestling, East Sussex TN35 4ET

Designed by Helen James
Edited by Mary-Jane Wilkins
Illustrated by Michael Woods

ISBN 0 7496 6730 3

Dewey Classification: 599.79'75

A CIP catalogue for this book is available from the British Library

Photographs by Alamy (Euroshots), Getty Images (LE Baskow, Tobias Bernhard, Cousteau Society,
Jason Edwards/National Geographic, Richard I'Anson, Romilly Lockyer, Don MacKinnon, Joseph Van Os,
Joel Sartore, Robert F. Sisson/National Geographic, Daniela Stolfi, James A. Sugar/National Geographic,
Medford Taylor/National Geographic, Art Wolfe, Konrad Wothe)

Printed and bound in Thailand

Contents

Sea lions

Sea lions look at home in the ocean as they bob up and down in the waves. You wouldn't guess that they are mammals related to land animals such as bears and dogs.

A sea lion is perfectly shaped for life in the water. It has a plump, streamlined body that narrows to a rounded nose at one end and a small tail at the other. Its body is covered with short brown fur that is slightly oily to make it waterproof.

Male sea lions are much larger than females. Full-grown males have a bony bump on the top of the forehead.

Most of the sea lions in zoos are California sea lions. These noisy, playful animals are very intelligent and easy to train.

A sea lion has four flippers, which it uses as paddles when it swims. Male sea lions are three or four times heavier than females and have darker brown fur.

Sea lions are fast, very graceful swimmers.

Sea lions and seals

Both seals and sea lions live in the sea and have flippers instead of legs. You might find it hard to tell them apart, but there are differences between them.

Sea lion

Seal

Sea lions can use their back flippers like legs to move faster and more easily on land than seals.

A sea lion moves much better on land because
it can tuck its back flippers underneath its body.
A seal can only wriggle along on land.

Another difference is that a sea lion has little earflaps
on both sides of its head. In fact, sometimes sea lions
are called eared seals. All you can see of a seal's ears
are small holes with no flaps.

**Can you see the little earflaps on the
sides of the heads of these sea lions?**

You're much more
likely to see sea
lions than seals in
a zoo. Some zoos
have fur seals,
but they are a
type of sea lion,
and not true seals.

At home in the wild

Sea lions usually swim and hunt in shallow waters close to coasts. They like to be near rocks and beaches where they can haul themselves out and take a rest from the sea.

California sea lions live along the Pacific coast of North America and around the Galápagos Islands. Other sea lions live further north, and on the coasts of South America, Australia and New Zealand.

Sea lions on a rocky Californian island.

Sea lions have a thick layer of fat called blubber under their skin that keeps them warm in cold water.

Sea lions like to bask in the warm sun.

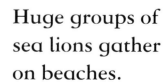

Huge groups of sea lions gather on beaches.

At home in the zoo

Sea lions are very popular zoo animals.
Many visitors love to watch them
playing and being fed.

Windows into the sea lions' enclosure allow visitors
to see how the animals behave underwater.

Most good zoos give sea lions
plenty of room to swim and dive.

Sea lions are friendly and like company, so good zoos keep
groups of them together. They need a large pool – saltwater
is best – and rocks and beaches to clamber on. Some zoos
even have a wave machine, which can be fun for the
animals. Many zoo sea lions were born in the zoo. Others
may have been injured or have lost their parents in the wild.

Life in the water

California sea lions can speed through the water at 20 km per hour, but they usually swim more slowly. They beat their front flippers up and down like wings to push themselves along, and steer with their back flippers.

Front flipper

Sea lions are expert divers and can stay underwater for at least three minutes, and sometimes as long as nine minutes.

Back flipper

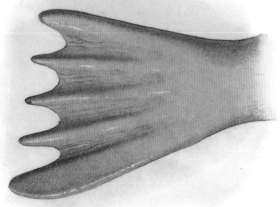

A sea lion has two front flippers and two back flippers. There are three claws on each back flipper.

When a sea lion dives, it keeps its nostrils and ears tightly closed so water doesn't get into them. Its heart beats more slowly while it is underwater. This means that the sea lion uses the air in its body more slowly than when it is on land.

After a rest on the rocks, sea lions like to dive and splash in the waves.

A sea lion's day

Sea lions spend two-thirds of their day at sea, swimming and diving, chasing fish and eating. They are active during the day and at night.

They spend the rest of the time on land. Sea lions like lots of company and gather in huge groups on rocks and beaches. They lie close together, sometimes even on top of each other. While on land they groom their sleek fur.

Sea lions spend much of their time on land grooming – licking their coat to keep it clean.

Sea lions in a zoo don't need to hunt, but they still spend a lot of time swimming and playing in the water.

 Can you spot the male? He is the big animal at the centre of this group of steller sea lions.

Sea lions scratch themselves with the nails on their back flippers, or rub their coats with their front flippers. Once a year sea lions moult – they lose their fur and grow new coats.

This sea lion is scratching an itch with the nails on its back flipper.

Feeding time

Sea lions are carnivores, like dogs and cats are on land. That means they live by killing and eating other creatures.

Sea lions are expert underwater hunters and feed on 50 different kinds of fish. They catch herring, mackerel and even small sharks, as well as squid and octopus.

Sea lions like to swim into a group of fish and snap up as many as they can.

Keepers usually feed zoo sea lions twice a day. A zoo sea lion may eat as much as 18 kg of fish a day – that's about 36 average-sized fish! Some trainers teach sea lions to beg or do tricks for food.

Sea lions find most of their food in shallow water during short dives lasting about two minutes. They also have enemies, or predators, in the ocean. Great white sharks and killer whales both attack sea lions.

California sea lions have between 34 and 38 teeth. They are shaped to catch and hold slippery fish rather than to chew.

Baby sea lions

California sea lion pups are born on land in the early summer. Sea lion mothers usually give birth to just one pup.

A newborn sea lion is plump and furry. Its eyes are open and it can move half an hour after birth. It can swim too, but not very well. The pup feeds on its mother's milk, which is rich and fatty so the pup grows fast.

A newborn sea lion pup weighs more than twice as much as a human baby.

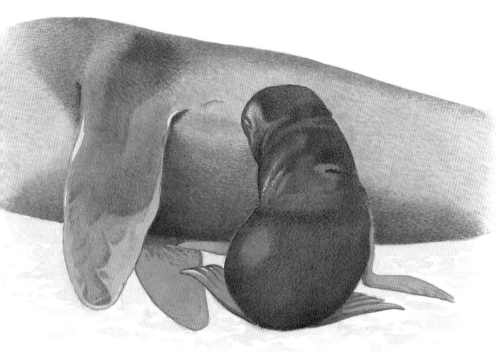

A sea lion mother in the wild would find it hard to rear two young. But sea lions in zoos sometimes give birth to twins. The mother needs a quiet area, away from visitors, where she can feel safe with her young.

A California sea lion pup feeds on its mother's milk for up to a year. The pup also eats fish once it is a few months old.

A mother sea lion will defend her pup fiercely against other animals. She stays with it all day and all night for about a week before she goes back to the sea to find food for herself.

Growing up

By the time sea lion pups are two or three weeks old their mothers are going to sea for several days at a time to feed.

Young sea lion pups call to their mums.

While their mums are away the pups gather in big groups called pods. When a mother comes back to land she calls loudly to her pup. A pup can tell its mother's call and bleats in reply. They keep calling until they find each other, when the mother gives her pup a quick sniff to check it really is hers before feeding it. Each pup has its own special smell.

Pups start to find some of their own food when they are four or five months old. They learn how to hunt by watching grown-up sea lions and copying them.

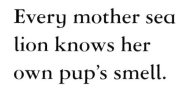

Sea lion pups play together from the age of about two or three weeks.

Every mother sea lion knows her own pup's smell.

Keeping in touch

Sea lions are amazingly noisy. On the rocks or the beach they bark and honk at one another constantly. They call to each other in the sea, too, and always seem to have something to say.

Pups make a high-pitched shriek when they are frightened and sea lions also grunt and growl.

The animals gather on land to mate, and each male has his own area, called a territory. They patrol this to defend it from other males, and bark loudly all the time. The big males also warn off others by shaking their heads and lunging at one another.

Male sea lions battle for territory on a beach. They start by roaring and pushing chest to chest. Then they may begin to snap and bite.

 Sea lions bark like dogs when they are in the sea as well as on land.

Playtime

Sea lions always look as though they're having fun in the water, and young animals love to play. Some play is practice for adult life. Young males have play fights which help to prepare them to defend their territory when they are grown up.

Sea lions are curious about scuba divers and often swim up to them for a closer look.

Zoo sea lions have plenty of toys to keep them busy. These include balls, floating logs and rafts to climb on and push around. Blocks of ice or balls containing fish are put in the enclosure so the animals have to work out how to get the food.

Young sea lions wrestle and chase each other in the water or push each other off rocks. Sea lions are also expert surfers and love to ride the waves and the wash behind boats.

They will pick up a bit of driftwood or a pebble, throw it into the air and catch it again and again. Sea lions also play with food, throwing and catching fish before eating them.

A sea lion leaps out of the water.

Sea lion senses

A sea lion relies on its senses to find food, like all animals. Hearing is especially important, and it can hear sounds in water that humans cannot. On land, sea lions don't hear as well as animals such as dogs and bears.

A sea lion's long whiskers sense tiny movements in the water, and help it to find prey.

Big round eyes help a sea lion see well, even in dim light. On either side of a sea lion's nose are 20-30 sensitive whiskers which it uses to find out about objects in water and on land.

A sea lion's sense of smell is poor in water but very good on land. It can smell humans from a great distance and females and pups know each other's special smell.

Sea lions probably live for 15-25 years in the wild. Animals in zoos and aquariums sometimes live as long as 30 years.

Sea lion fact file

Here is some more information about sea lions.
Your mum or dad might like to read this, or
you could read these pages together.

A sea lion is a mammal, but it spends much of its time in water
and is so well suited to this life that it has flippers instead of legs.

Where sea lions live
There are five kinds of sea lion in different parts of the world.

California sea lion: coasts of California and the
   Galápagos Islands in the Pacific Ocean
Northern or steller sea lion: North Pacific coasts
South American or southern sea lion: Atlantic and
   Pacific coasts of South America
Australian sea lion: Australian coasts
New Zealand sea lion: New Zealand coasts

Fur seals are close relatives of sea lions. There are nine kinds of
fur seal living on South American and African coasts, as well
as around subantarctic islands and New Zealand. Like sea lions,
fur seals have little ear flaps and can tuck their back flippers
under their bodies to move on land.

Sea lion numbers

There are lots of most kinds of sea lion and probably about 250,000 California sea lions. However, large numbers of sea lions are hurt by pollution in the ocean and accidentally caught in fishing nets.

Size

Male sea lions are between 2.3 and 2.8 metres long and weigh 250 to 600 kilograms. Females are 1.5 to 2.2 metres long and weigh 80 to 270 kilograms. The northern or steller sea lion is the biggest kind.

Find out more

If you want to know more about sea lions, check out these websites.

Fort Wayne Children's Zoo
http://www.kidszoo.com/animals/sealion.htm

Seaworld
http://www.seaworld.org/animal-info/info-books/california-sea-lion/index.htm

The Marine Mammal Center
http://www.marinemammalcenter.org/learning/education/pinnipeds/casealion.asp

The Big Zoo
http://www.thebigzoo.com/Animals/California_Sea_Lion.asp

Words to remember

blubber
A thick layer of fat under the sea lion's skin which helps keep it warm in cold water.

carnivore
A mammal that eats the flesh of other animals.

colony
A big group of animals gathered together in one place.

enclosure
The area where an animal lives in a zoo.

flippers
A sea lion has flippers instead of arms and legs. The flippers are shaped like paddles to help it move through water.

grooming
Cleaning fur to remove dirt and insects.

mammal
A warm-blooded animal, usually with four legs and some hair on its body. Sea lions have flippers instead of legs. Female mammals feed their babies with milk from their own bodies.

mate
To produce babies.

moult
To lose fur and grow a new coat.

predators
Animals that hunt other animals to eat.

territory
An animal's special area that it defends from other animals.

Index